PIANO REPERTOIRE
MELODIOUS MASTERPIECES
Book 1

Compiled and Edited by Jane Magrath

▼▼▼▼▼▼▼▼▼▼▼▼▼▼▼▼▼▼▼▼▼▼▼▼▼▼▼▼▼▼▼▼▼▼▼

CONTENTS

▲▲▲▲▲▲▲▲▲▲▲▲▲▲

▼▼▼▼▼▼▼▼▼▼▼▼▼▼▼

This book is dedicated to
Anna Kwa.

Jane Magrath

Cover Illustration: David Cristiana

▼▼

▼▼

Suggested Teaching Order

This ordering is only suggested and is designed primarily as an overall gauge of difficulty.

1 **Spindler** *Song without Words*
2 **Bertini** *Chord Study*, Op. 166, No. 6
3 **Gurlitt** *Melodic Study*, Op. 50, No. 5
4 **Duncombe** *Sonatina in C Major*
5 **Schumann** *Melody*, Op. 68, No. 1
6 **Kabalevsky** *Song*, Op. 27, No. 2
7 **Gurlitt** *The Bright Sky*, Op. 140, No. 3
8 **Gurlitt** *Song without Words*, Op. 117, No. 34
9 **Clementi** *Arietta in C Major*
10 **Mozart** *Minuet in C Major*, K. 6
11 **Gurlitt** *Slumber Song*, Op. 101, No. 6
12 **Gurlitt** *Allegretto*, Op. 50, No. 6
13 **Gurlitt** *The Little Wanderer*, Op. 140, No. 13
14 **Kuhnau** *Prelude in G Major*
15 **Tchaikovsky** *In Church*, Op. 39, No. 23
16 **Schumann** *First Loss*, Op. 68, No. 16
17 **Tchaikovsky** *Old French Song*, Op. 39, No. 16
18 **Gurlitt** *By the Spring*, Op. 101, No. 5
19 **Rebikov** *Gather Around the Christmas Tree*

20 **Scarlatti** *Sonata in C Major*, K. 73b
21 **Köhler** *The Child Asleep*, Op. 283, No. 22
22 **Heller** *Etude in C Major*, Op. 47, No. 19
23 **Scarlatti** *Aria*, K. 32
24 **Gretchaninoff** *My Dear Mother*, Op. 119, No. 1
25 **Gurlitt** *The Murmuring Brook*, Op. 140, No. 5
26 **Tchaikovsky** *Morning Prayer*, Op. 39, No. 1
27 **Rebikov** *Angels*
28 **Tchaikovsky** *Daydream*, Op. 39, No. 21
29 **Gretchaninoff** *Nurse Tells a Story*, Op. 119, No. 8
30 **Maykapar** *The Orphan*, Op. 28, No. 2
31 **Bach** *Musette in G Major*
32 **Kabalevsky** *A Melancholic Rain*, Op. 89, No. 34
33 **Kabalevsky** *At the River*, Op. 89, No. 35
34 **Gurlitt** *Longing*, Op. 140, No. 11
35 **Schumann** *The Reaper's Song*, Op. 68, No. 18
36 **Heller** *Tolling Bell*, Op. 125, No. 8
37 **Khachaturian** *Andantino*
38 **Heller** *Prelude in C Minor*, Op. 119, No. 25

▼▼

Preface

▲▲▲▲▲▲▲▲▲▲▲▲▲

As the title reflects, the pieces found in this anthology are *Melodious.* Included are both familiar and less familiar pieces, all of which require the performer to play in a lyrical manner. Many of these pieces call for a refined control of the melodic line and skill in phrasing. Many will also advance the performer's skill in voicing a melody above an accompaniment. They are pieces that should motivate and inspire the performer. Various compositional styles are represented with an intentionally strong representation of literature from the Romantic period. It is the Romantic period literature that provides a great wealth of music that is *Melodious.* This Romantic period music often still remains little known and little represented in today's teaching collections.

All works are original compositions presented in their original version and based on primary editions when possible. Editing has been kept to a minimum so that the essence of the composer's original text stands out. Most fingerings are editorial as are dynamic indications in the Baroque and, sparingly, in the Classical selections. All suggestions strive to steer the performer in the direction of the most authoritative and stylistically appropriate performance possible.

Students capable of playing standard classical literature from *Masterwork Classics*, Books 3–5 (easiest pieces by Haydn and Mozart, easiest works from the *Anna Magdalena Bach Notebook* and Gurlitt's *Album for the Young*, Op. 140) may work from this volume. A suggested teaching order is provided only as a guide to assigning repertoire in this collection. The performer may also enjoy investigating literature in the companion volume to this one, *Piano Repertoire … Masterpieces With Flair!*, Book 1, also published by Alfred Publishing Company.

The editor extends warm thanks and appreciation to Morty and Iris Manus for their insight, help, encouragement and continuous support. Appreciation for their help is also due to Kim O'Reilly and David Smooke.

Practice Notes

▲▲▲▲▲▲▲▲▲▲▲▲▲

BACH

A musette is a work of pastoral character with a sustained drone. Note the long drone in this musette. A true finger legato in both hands is essential for an effective performance of this work. Careful practice of each hand independently, from the outset of study, will pay off in a solidly learned fingering that makes a true *legatissimo* possible.

CLEMENTI

The two-note slurs render this a highly expressive work from the Classical era. Portray a strong feeling of tension and release in these slurs, especially in measure 16. Use finger legato when possible to maintain a seamless sound.

DUNCOMBE

Strive for a strong pulse in this stately work. Maintain smooth and inaudible finger crossings under and over the thumb.

KUHNAU

During the Baroque period, works similar to this piece containing broken chords might have been composed for the lute, a forerunner of the modern guitar, as well as for a keyboard instrument. The performer might imagine how this piece would sound if it were played on a guitar. This work provides ample opportunity to listen for harmonic tension and release.

▼▼

MOZART

This elegant work was composed when Mozart was a child. Again, the feeling of tension and release is an essential component of the musical framework. Listen carefully to the releases of all phrases.

SCARLATTI

Played in a highly expressive way, this aria can be an emotional showstopper. The two-note slurs throughout lend a melancholic flavor and provide fine opportunity for a highly expressive performance. A refined finger legato, especially in the right hand, can help control the melodic line. Although originally conceived for the harpsichord, this expressive work is especially effectively on the modern piano.

This lyrical sonata progresses through a series of sequences and harmonic shifts. The harmonic changes help determine the interpretation. Strive for a feeling of one pulse in each measure. This work can be memorized easily by discovering the patterns throughout. Note the various chords outlined in the right hand as well as the different intervallic structures. A true finger legato in the left hand is necessary.

BERTINI

This harplike piece is based on a harmonic progression of chords similar to that in the Kuhnau *Prelude in G Major*. Strive to match the tone quality between the hands as one hand takes over from the other. An overlapping finger legato is acceptable in this work.

GURLITT

The broken chords should roll from hand to hand seamlessly throughout this harmonic study. Let the first bass note of each measure project slightly as a harmonic foundation for the measure. The performer may want to finger pedal, or hold slightly longer than notated, the first bass note of each measure.

The performer has a fine opportunity to display a true singing tone in this *grazioso* work. The accompanying Alberti bass needs to be voiced under the melody. Avoid the tendency for the high melodic notes reached by skip to protrude from the texture.

The melody in *By the Spring* is based on short motives that require subtle musical inflection throughout. Strive to maintain a loose and relaxed wrist and to sink into the key in an attempt to achieve a warm and singing tone.

This graceful character piece calls for careful inflection of the short melodic phrases. The abundant repetition of ideas in this ABABA–form work provides a compact amount of material to learn.

This work seems to portray a feeling of striving for something. Notice the way in which the melody tends to reach (skip) upward as if grasping for some feeling or thought. Throughout, the right hand must balance the playing of both the melody and accompaniment, both of which should be voiced appropriately. The extensive repetition in this work reduces the amount of time necessary to learn it.

▼▼

In this broken-chord study, strive to match the tone quality between the hands as the line moves from one hand to the other. This is also a fine study for listening to the harmonic progressions and interpreting accordingly. Play each phrase as a single musical thought.

Gurlitt establishes a character reminiscent of water murmuring in a small brook or stream with busy 16th-note activity within a soft dynamic range. This piece is an excellent study in gaining skill in voicing two lines within one hand. Throughout, the performer must bring out the melody while subduing the accompaniment in the same hand. Note the frequent repetition of ideas in this short work.

The melodic duet between the right and left hands can be enchanting in this Romantic character piece. The melody requires shading and shaping throughout; be sure to match tone quality in the melodic line.

Song without Words is a hand-to-hand, broken-chord study. Notice that the first note in each hand is double-stemmed. That indicates that this note should be held for the longer value notated and that this note should be brought out as a melody note.

HELLER

This etude is a study in tonal control, composed to help a performer achieve the ability to play with a singing tone. The accents notated in the score should be interpreted generally as notes that should be emphasized or stress, not accented, within the melody. Lean slightly on these notes because the music often seems to pull to those points. Some use of overlapping legato is appropriate.

This enchanting work provides an opportunity to hear the rich and lush quality of various full harmonies. Maintain a loose and supple wrist throughout to help achieve a singing tone. Continue to work on voicing the texture to the tops of the chords. Maintain strong intensity in the section immediately prior to the return of the A-section material at measure 29.

The tolling of a bell is depicted in the sustained tones throughout, often appearing in the left hand. Let these tones ring out. The eighth-note accompaniment needs to move forward musically. The use of overlapping legato in some of the right-hand broken-chord passages is appropriate. Syncopated pedaling should be used throughout. Listen carefully to help achieve clear changes of the pedal.

KÖHLER

The narrow dynamic range of this piece, mostly within a *p* to *pp* spectrum, calls for fine control of tone and skillful inflection of the motivic ideas. The harmonic movement determines the musical plan for this work. Perform *The Child Asleep* at a tempo that allows the feeling of one pulse per measure.

▼▼

SCHUMANN

The descending two-note slurs lend a flavor of melancholy or remembrance of something special that has been lost. *First Loss* is built on many short motives, all of which need shading and finesse. Note the contrapuntal entrances of the melodic material in measures 20, 21 and 22. These entrances should be projected clearly.

Strive to achieve a seamless legato in this lyrical work. The treble G's in the left hand need to be subdued within the accompanimental texture.

Strive to portray the feeling of slightly more movement in the B section beginning in measure 13 to contrast with the more relaxed feeling of the A sections. Voicing of the melody above the thick texture is essential.

SPINDLER

This highly lyrical work calls for a singing tone in the right hand and subdued broken-chord accompaniment in the left. Listen attentively and try to match the melodic tones evenly. The right-hand melody should project above the accompaniment.

TCHAIKOVSKY

Imagine one's feelings as one daydreams and becomes lost in thoughts and moods. In this reflective and introspective piece, the performer should focus on bringing out the duet in the outer voices and projecting the melodic line while keeping the off-beat accompanimental chords quiet. Strive here, as in other works, to achieve a seamless legato with evenly matched tones.

This programmatic work reflects the chorale-like textures of organ music often heard in churches; the mood is solemn. The performer should strive to voice out the tops of the chords and maintain a finger legato whenever possible.

An important aspect of playing this chordal work is the finger connection of various voices from chord to chord. Although the damper pedal should be used, avoid relying on it as a substitute for finger legato. Strive to voice out the tops of the chords. The concluding section, measures 17 to the end, needs careful voicing of the low, thick registers. Keep the G pedal point in the bass moving forward musically.

Old French Song needs careful inflection and shaping of the melodic motives. Maintain this shaping in the section beginning at measure 17, in which the left hand provides a staccato accompaniment to the sustained right-hand melody.

GRETCHANINOFF

The sentimental melody here is perhaps reflective of a tender memory of one's mother. The upward skips in the melody should be matched in tone with the rest of the melody.

A pleasant remembrance from childhood can be depicted through the performance of this lyrical work. Strive for skillful and appropriate voicing of melody and accompaniment in the right hand. The repeated material expedites the learning process.

▼▼

KABALEVSKY

This eerie and powerful work calls for ringing tones in both hands. Avoid a tempo that is too fast, striving instead to maintain the languid and dispirited mood that prevails throughout.

The left-hand accompaniment here depicts a melancholy rainfall and the consistent dripping of the rain. For an effective performance, strive to contrast strongly the lyrical melody with the secco accompaniment.

This simple, lyrical work calls for a singing tone in the melody voiced above the accompaniment. Observe carefully the phrasing marked in the score.

KHACHATURIAN

Play the melody of this work with a smooth legato in which the fingers almost overlap one another. This lyrical work consists of a main theme stated in measures 1–9, an extension or variation of the melody in measures 10–17, a variation of the accompaniment to the melody in measures 18–25, and a coda in measures 26–29. Notice the many left-hand patterns, whose discovery makes the work easier to learn. Be sure to maintain a singing melodic tone throughout.

MAYKAPAR

This expressive work is set primarily in the upper register of the piano. Strive to maintain the rhythmic movement of the melody toward points of tension and achieve a seamless legato.

REBIKOV

In this work, as in the following one, strive to voice out the top notes in the right-hand double-note passages. In this piece also, the top notes are the melody. Although this piece contains many short passages under slurs, be sure to play long phrases throughout.

Strive to bring out the top melody notes in the right hand chords.

This page has been left blank in order to eliminate an awkward page turn.

Sonata in C Major

Domenico Scarlatti (1685–1757)
K. 73b

Aria

Domenico Scarlatti (1685–1757)
K. 32

* The editor suggests that the left-hand chords in measures 1, 3, 5, 11, 17 and 21
  be rolled or arpeggiated from the bottom upward.

Prelude in G Major

Johann Kuhnau
(1660–1722)

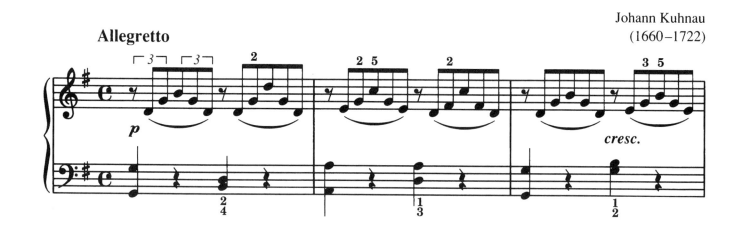

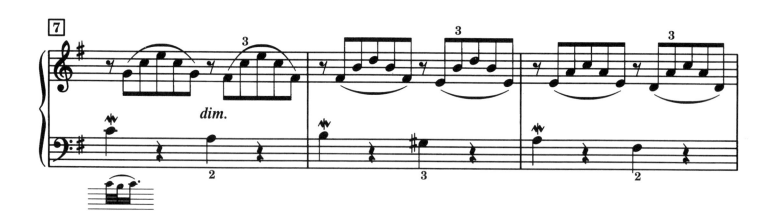

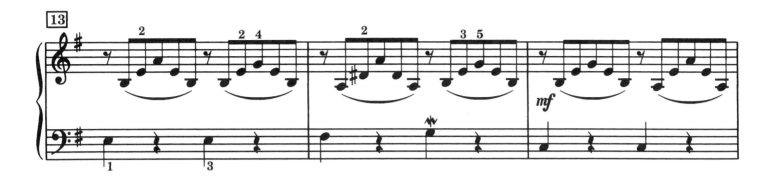

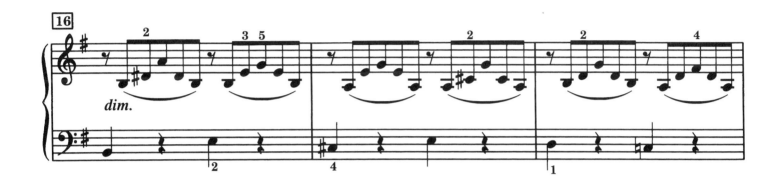

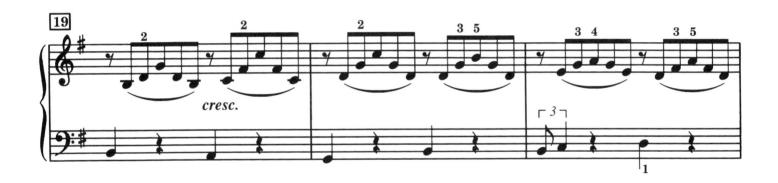

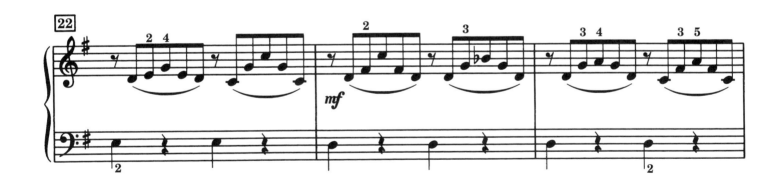

Musette in G Major

Johann Sebastian Bach
(1685–1750)

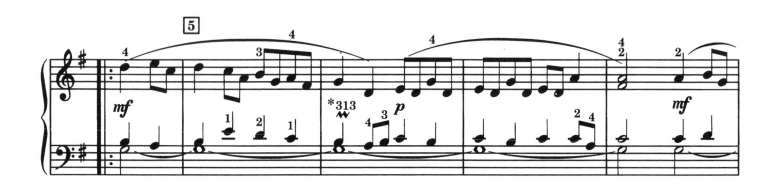

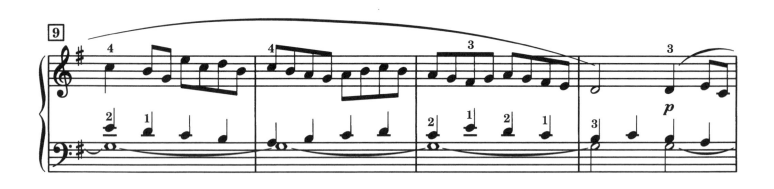

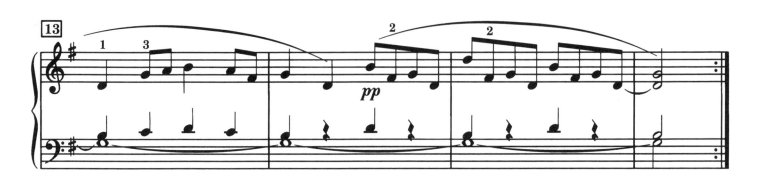

* Ornament is optional.

Sonatina in C Major

William Duncombe
(1690–1769)

Arietta in C Major

Muzio Clementi
(1752–1832)

Minuet in C Major

W. A. Mozart (1756–1791)
K. 6

Chord Study

Henri Bertini (1798–1876)
Op. 166, No. 6

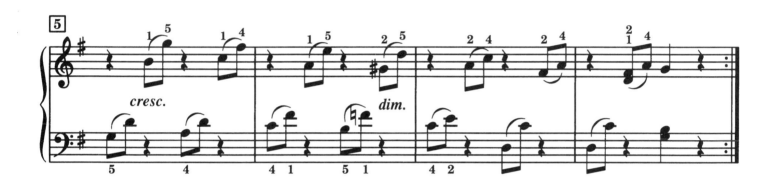

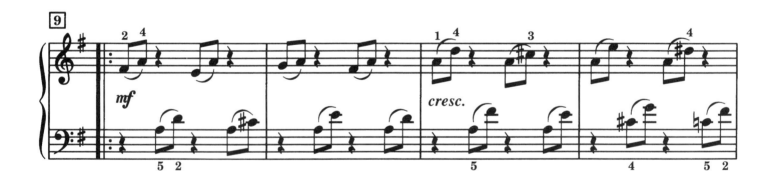

Song without Words

Fritz Spindler
(1817–1905)

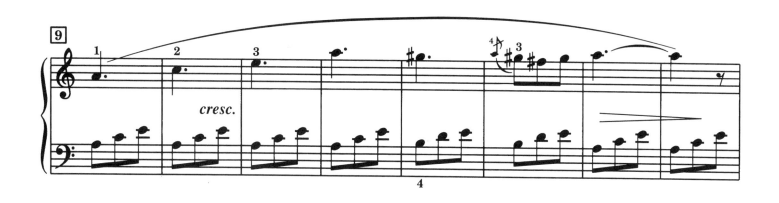

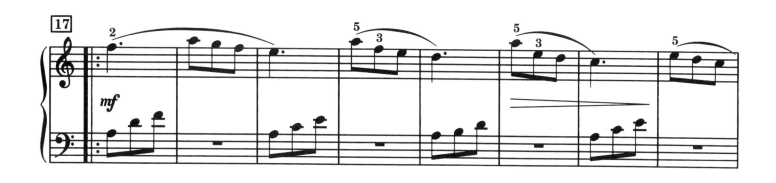

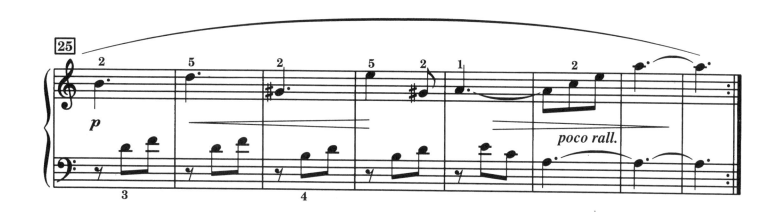

The Bright Sky

Cornelius Gurlitt (1820–1901)
Op. 140, No. 3

Allegretto grazioso

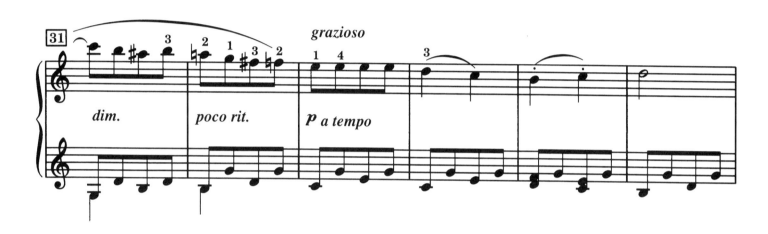

Slumber Song

Cornelius Gurlitt (1820–1901)
Op. 101, No. 6

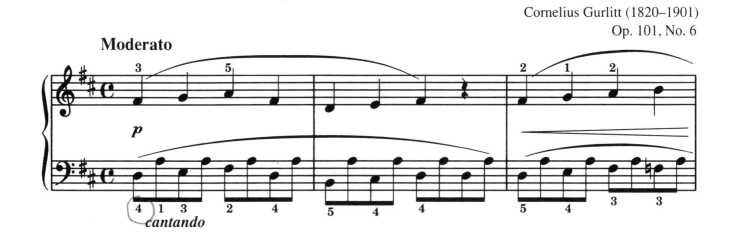

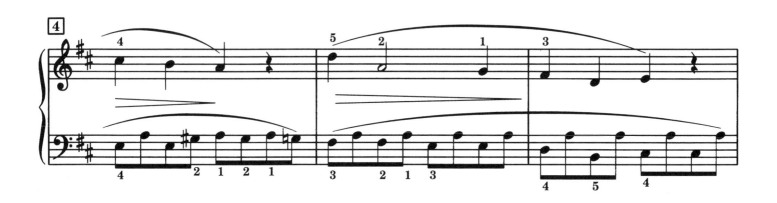

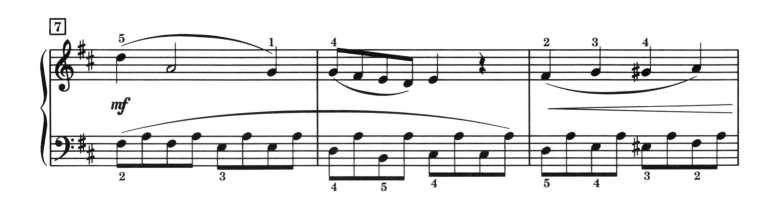

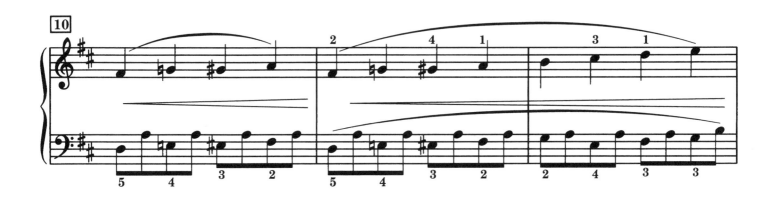

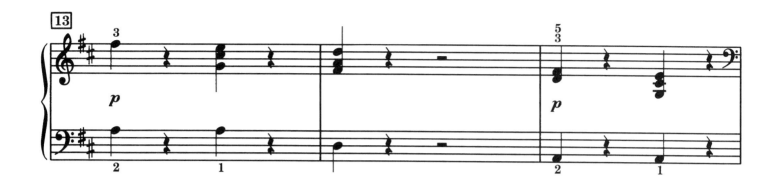

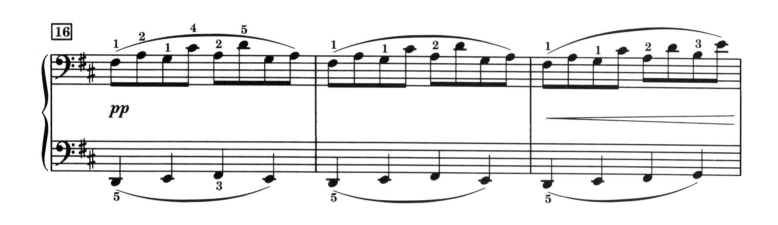

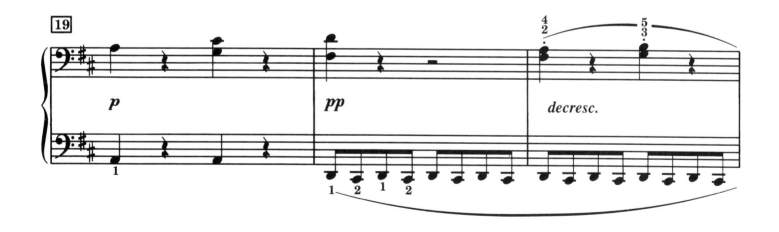

Song without Words

Cornelius Gurlitt (1820–1901)
Op. 117, No. 34

24

By the Spring

Cornelius Gurlitt (1820–1901)
Op. 101, No. 5

Moderato, quasi Allegretto

Longing

Cornelius Gurlitt (1820–1901)
Op. 140, No. 11

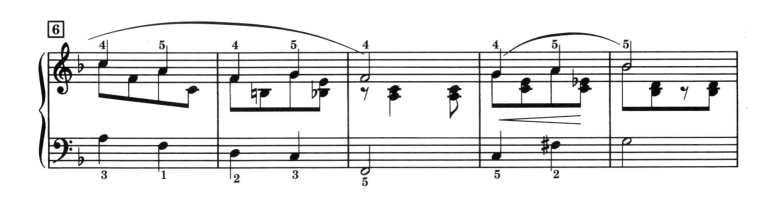

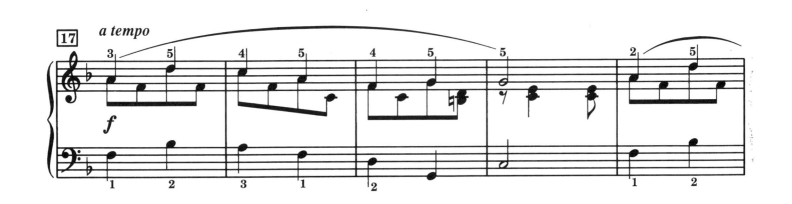

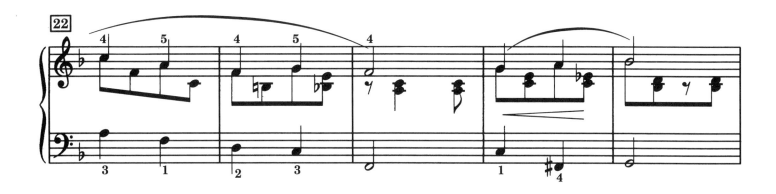

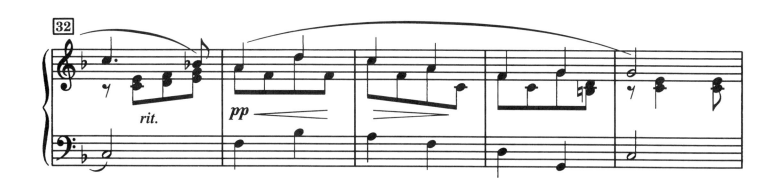

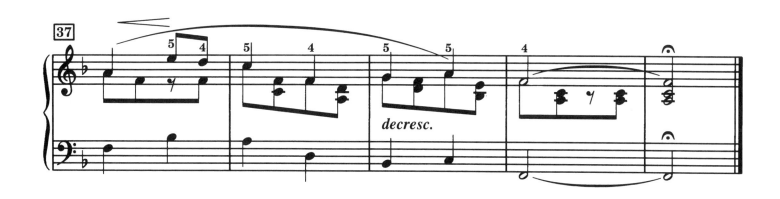

Allegretto

Cornelius Gurlitt (1820–1901)
Op. 50, No. 6

The Little Wanderer

Cornelius Gurlitt (1820–1901)
Op. 140, No. 13

The Murmuring Brook

Cornelius Gurlitt (1820–1901)
Op. 140, No. 5

Con moto

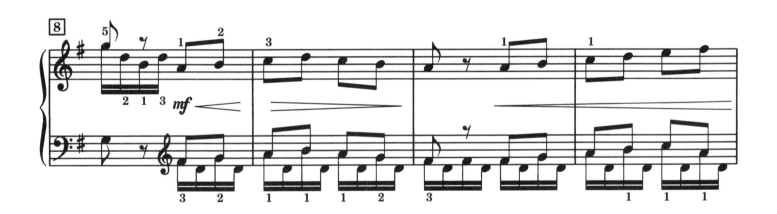

Melodic Study

Cornelius Gurlitt (1820–1901)
Op. 50, No. 5

Melody

Robert Schumann (1810 –1856)
Op. 68, No. 1

First Loss

Robert Schumann (1810–1856)
Op. 68, No. 16

The Reaper's Song

(Not very fast)
Nicht sehr schnell

Robert Schumann (1810–1856)
Op. 68, No. 18

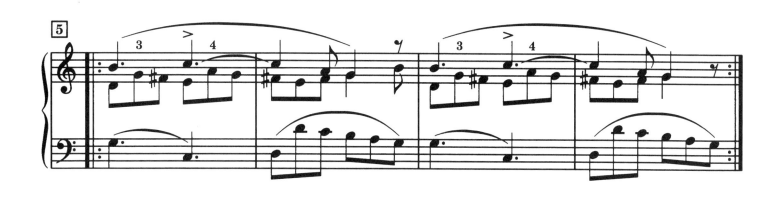

Morning Prayer

Peter Ilyich Tchaikovsky (1840–1893)
Op. 39, No. 1

Daydream

Peter Ilyich Tchaikovsky (1840–1893)
Op. 39, No. 21

In Church

Peter Ilyich Tchaikovsky (1840–1893)
Op. 39, No. 23*

Moderato

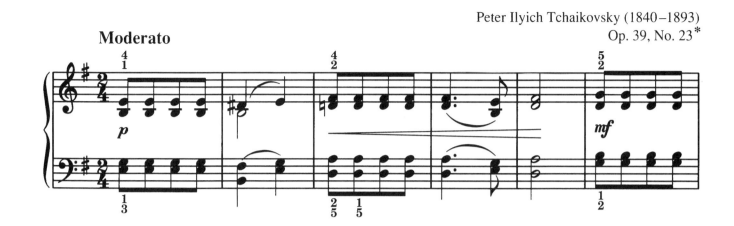

* Although many collections cite this work as Op. 39, No. 24, Tchaikovsky originally listed it as No. 23. Tchaikovsky's original ordering was slightly altered by a publisher.

Old French Song

Peter Ilyich Tchaikovsky (1840–1893)
Op. 39, No. 16

Tolling Bell

Stephen Heller (1813–1888)
Op. 125, No. 8

Etude in C Major

Stephen Heller (1813–1888)
Op. 47, No. 19

Prelude in C Minor

Stephen Heller (1813–1888)
Op. 119, No. 25

The Child Asleep

Louis Köhler (1820–1886)
Op. 283, No. 22

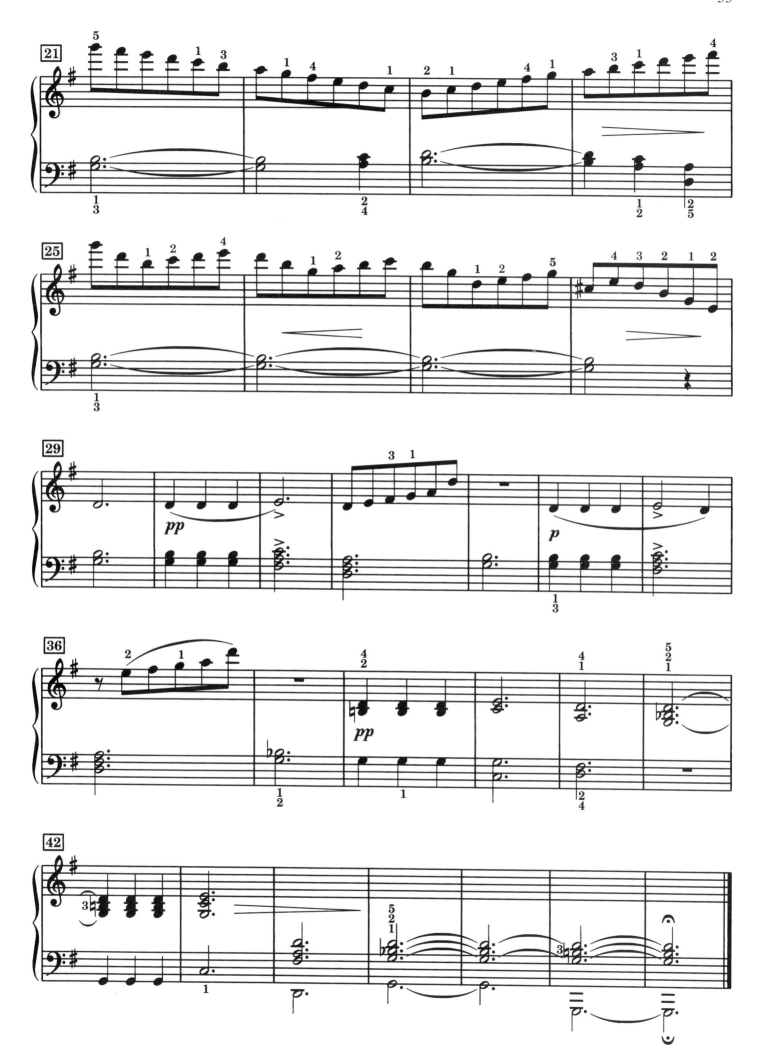

Nurse Tells a Story

Alexander Gretchaninoff (1864 –1956)
Op. 119, No. 8

My Dear Mother

Alexander Gretchaninoff (1864–1956)
Op. 119, No. 1

Gather Around the Christmas Tree

Vladimir Rebikov
(1866–1920)

Angels

Vladimir Rebikov
(1866–1920)

The Orphan

Samuel Maykapar (1867–1938)
Op. 28, No. 2

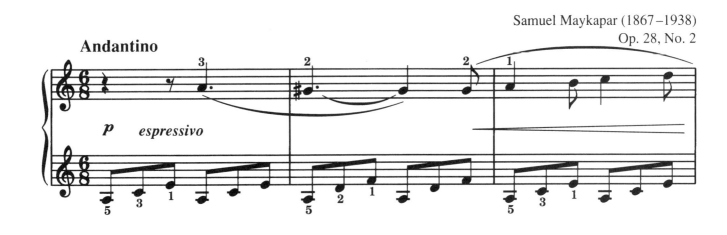

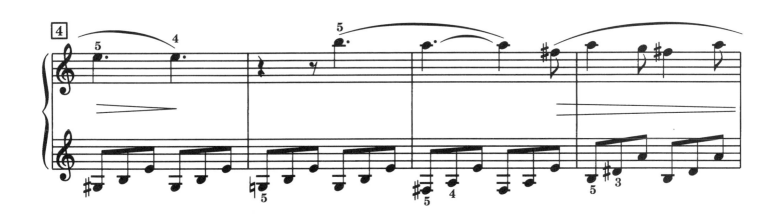

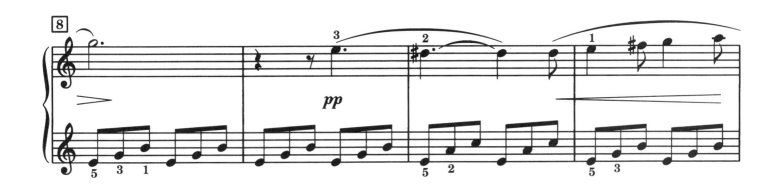

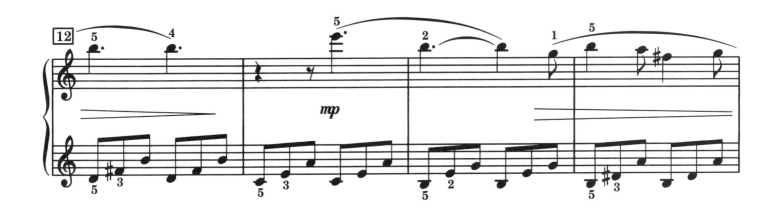

Andantino

Aram Khachaturian
(1903–1978)

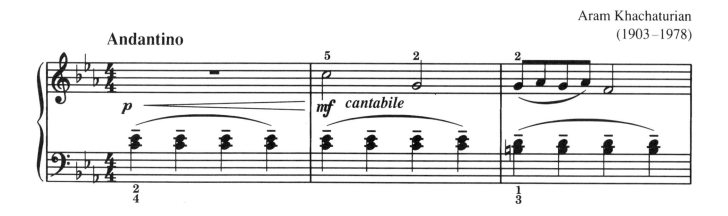

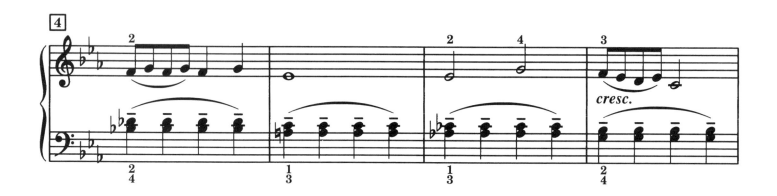

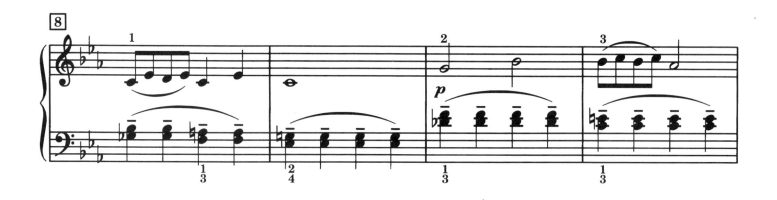

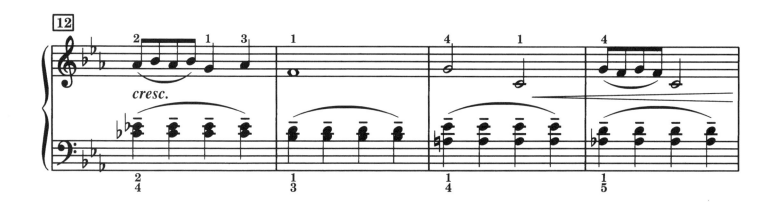

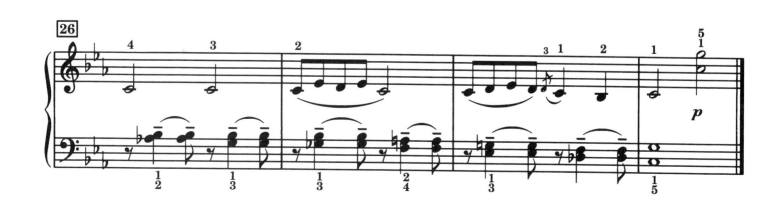

Song

Dmitri Kabalevsky (1904–1987)
Op. 27, No. 2

A Melancholic Rain

Dmitri Kabalevsky (1904–1987)
Op. 89, No. 34

At the River

Dmitri Kabalevsky (1904–1987)
Op. 89, No. 35